Hello! How are you?

Since 2017, our group of faculty and students from the State University of Santa Catarina (UDESC) in Southern Brazil has been offering theatre workshops inside the women's prison in the city of Florianópolis. In Portuguese our group is called ***Teatro e Prisão: práticas de infiltração das artes cênicas em espaços de vigilânça***, which in English would be something like Theatre and Prison: Practices of Performing Arts Infiltration in Detention Spaces. Our activities were suspended in 2020 at the start of the Covid-19 pandemic when volunteers were no longer allowed into the prison.

We developed this workbook as a way to stay connected to the women in the prison and to each other. We took inspiration from a project called ***Women with Possibilities*** (Mulheres Possiveis). We hope that this workbook can give us all a chance to breathe in these times, possibilities for self-perception and self-care, a space for expression, creation, and art making.

Our friends in the United States at the Prison Creative Arts Project (PCAP) at the University of Michigan asked our permission to translate this book into English and share it with people there. We are very glad that this book can now reach people in another nation and another language.

We would love to create with you in person, but when we cannot be together, we can still share these pages, words, images, and emotions.

May our words reach you like a hug, wrapped up in warmth!

____

write here the name you'd like to use

(it doesn't have to be your real name)

Conceived, organized, and written by
Professor Vicente Concilio (UDESC)
Professor Caroline Vetori (UDESC)

Edited by
Professor Anelise Zimmermann (UDESC)
Professor Sara Copetti Klohn (University of Rio Grande do Sul)

Graphic design by
Professor Anelise Zimmermann (UDESC)
Professor Sara Copetti Klohn (University of Rio Grande do Sul)
Clara Sohn (UDESC)
Fernanda Gonçalves (UDESC)

English translation by
Professor Ashley Lucas (University of Michigan)

Contact information for Teatro e Prisão: práticas de infiltração das artes cênicas em espaços de vigilânça
teatroeprisao@gmail.com

Contact information for the Prison Creative Arts Project
pcapinfo@umich.edu

Acknowledgements
This workbook is indebted to the university community engagement programs ***Programas de Extensão Pedagogia de Teatro e Processos de Criação*** and ***Entre livros, tipos e desenhos: interlocuções da cultura gráfica*** at the ***Centro das Artes*** at the ***Universidade do Estado de Santa Catarina*** (UDESC). It was printed in Brazil with resources from ***Edital PAEX-PROCEU/UDESC*** in 2020 and 2021, and the original edition in Portuguese was distributed in Brazil for free to people and organizations in the state of Santa Catarina.

The English edition was supported by the Public Engagement Faculty Fellows program at the University of Michigan, the UM Brazil Initiative, and Michigan Publishing Services. This edition was printed in Michigan and distributed for free in prisons throughout the state.

Call for Writing by Incarcerated Writers in Michigan

The ***Michigan Review of Prisoner Creative Writing*** showcases the talent and diversity of writers who are currently incarcerated in Michigan. This annual review serves as one facet of the University of Michigan's Prison Creative Arts Project, which brings those impacted by the justice system together with the University of Michigan community for artistic collaboration, mutual learning, and growth.
As PCAP's literary review, it features short stories, poems, essays, and maybe even short plays from both beginning and experienced writers. It offers writing that comes from the heart and is unique, well-crafted, and lively.
We can only accept submissions from people currently incarcerated in the state of Michigan.

The ***Michigan Review of Prisoner Creative Writing*** is accepting submissions of poetry, fictions, plays, and short essays year-round. We tend to do most of the reading during the school year, and acceptance/ rejection letters go out at the end of the semesters (so if you send something during the summer, you may not hear back about it until December). Please do not send novel- or novella-length works or other whole books, as we cannot publish them. Please accompany your submission with a note that includes any pen names you want us to use, your MDOC or BOP ID number, and your current address.

The place to send them is:

Attn: John F. Buckley
Prison Creative Arts Project
East Quad/Residential College
701 E. University Ave.
Ann Arbor, MI 48109-1245

Guidelines

1 There is no right or ~~wronge~~ wrong.

Play with the words. You can express yourself any way that you want. You can write or draw. This workbook is yours!

2 Reading is also an act of creation.

The way in which you understand an activity is the way it should be done. The exercises in this book can be reimagined in whatever way you read them, which is personal. That is to say, no one can do this for you.

3 Make adaptations.

Transform these exercises as you see fit in the moment. For example, if you wanted to write in purple but don't have that color ink, you could write a note in the margin, saying: "I would have liked to have written this in purple."

4 Try to get in touch with yourself and with others.

These words, these games can be precious keys. They can open heavy and difficult doors. They can transport us to other places.

5 Take your time.

Don't rush to finish the activities or the workbook. After each exercise, think about it. Notice how it moved you, what it did to you physically, sensorially, emotionally. If you can, share it with a partner. Talk about your feelings and listen to theirs.

6 Use the workbook like a diary of experiments, creations, and things you have learned.

Please include the date of each activity. It can be nice to know when you wrote something and track your progress over time.

7 You don't need to do the activities in order.

Do the activities in the order that you find most interesting.

Let's go!
We'll see you on the next page.

Planting Words

tomorrow is at the corner of time,
we will meet there soon
and come across a new path,
fresh starts,
new encounters,
that demand days of growth,
ancient calendars that open the leaves of the morning,
in the word hope there is waiting
let us wait and dance our dances

A blank page is a universe of possibilities to be created.

Here, symbolically, we invite you to create a new day.

Plant words that can be seeds!

Plant words—feelings—desires in this fertile ground.

put the date here!

__/__/__

A Letter for the Future

What would you like to say?
What are your **plans**, your **desires**, your **dreams**?
What advice would you give your future self?

Don't stop to think.
Let your thoughts turn
into **words** and/or **desires**
on the paper without judgement. . . Let it flow.

Write a letter to:

your future self

Dear self,

__/__/__

We Have Many Versions of Ourselves

When we introduce ourselves, we usually start with the phrase, **"I am..."**
It seems like a something definitive, but in reality we have **many versions of ourselves**, don't we?
Knowing how different we are at each moment can help us free ourselves from what people think of us because we know our existence can't be summed up in just being one thing...
Knowing this is what makes us **unique**...

This exercise was inspired by an activity book in Portuguese called Mulheres possíveis (Possible Women).

With this in mind, tell us:

Who are you?

Write small

W r i t e s l o w l y

Write fast

WRITE BIG

__/__/__

I Am, I Am Not

Complete the sentences with words or drawings:

I am

I am not

Everyone knows that

No one knows that

I want

I don't want

I play

I sing

If I were a book, I would be

If I were a color, I would be

__/__/__

If I were a color,
I would be
red.

I have

I know

I dream

I support

If I were

If I flew

If I were an object, I would be

If I

If I was a character, I would be

If I Could. . .

In the theatre, we often use
the magic **"if"**:

If I was another person?

If I could do anything?

The magic **"if"** helps us to fly into the universe of imagination, and it can be your best friend.

It helps us to imagine other situations and to travel the world.

What **if** we met face-to-face to get to know each other?

How would you introduce yourself?
What would you say about yourself?

And what would you ask?
What would you like to know?

Tell this story by writing about it.

 __/__/__

Hello, my name is

If I Found . . ....

Now, let's change the characters
and the location of this meeting a little.

Imagine **if** the person in front of you
was a very famous person
who wanted to interview you.

Who is this person interviewing you?

What is the purpose, context or location of the interview?
What questions does this famous person ask?

And how do you respond?

Here, we begin to play more with reality (you) and fiction (the famous person and the location of the interview).

You can respond with partial truths and also your own inventions. Play with fantasy.

Hello, we are here with...

__/__/__

Questions

Now, ask a friend
what they think would be interesting to ask
when **they meet someone for the first time.**

If possible, ask
other people and write down
what they say.

Write their suggestions here:

How was your day?

Now you have some different questions in your workbook, right?

Try responding to these same questions in your workbook.

__/__/__

What No One Ever Asked Me Before

What would you like to tell that **no one ever asked you about before?**

Write the questions and your responses.

__/__/__

Draw Yourself

Try to make a **self-portrait**. Have you ever drawn yourself? Try it here.

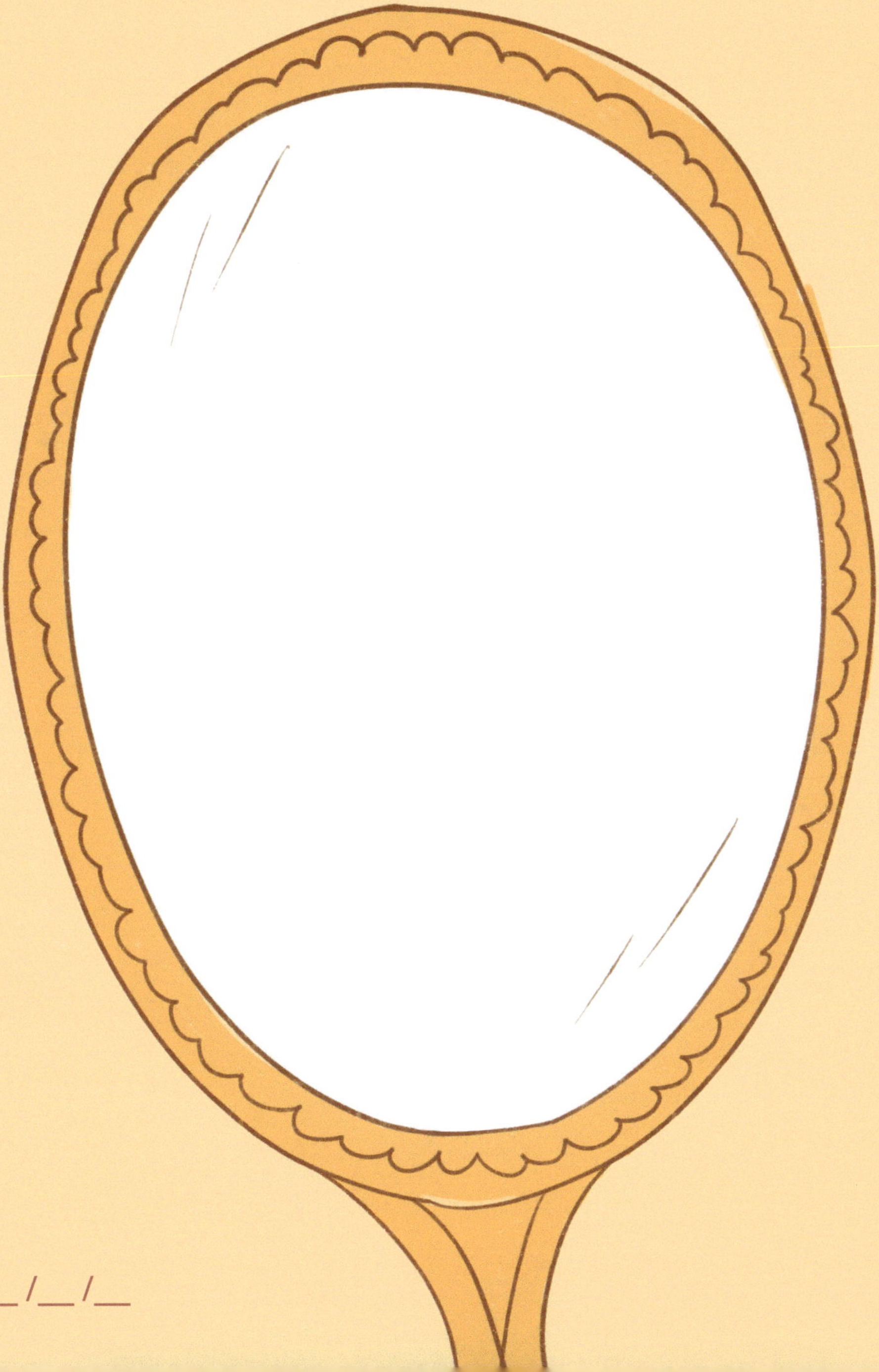

__/__/__

If I Were an Object

Think of an object that describes **you.**

Draw the object.

Now, write about this object, as if you were this object.

If I Were Water

> *The river that sweeps everything away*
> *is said to be violent.*
> *But no one says that*
> *the banks that channel it are violent.*
>
> Bertolt Brecht

Imagine that the **trajectory of your life** until now was made of water.

Draw your path,

thinking of the words:

Where is this water running to?

Was this water a river? A waterfall?
The sea? The rain?

Did this water run into dams?
Did it make rapids?

__/__/__

If I Were Rain

If we imagine that we are **drops of water**, we can pretend that other people are, too, and **when these drops meet**, they become rain, rivers, the sea, lakes, waterfalls, and rapids.

Discuss your life journey as a raindrop with some friends.

Write or draw these adventures.

What do you have in common?

What is different about each of you?

In what rivers did you meet?

I Become

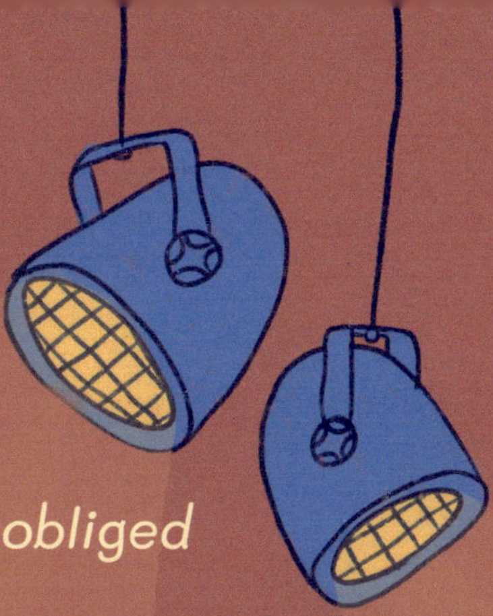

(...) why do I write?
I write, almost as if I were obliged
To find myself
While I write
I am not the Other
But the voice itself
Not the object
But the subject.
I become the one who describes
And not the one who is described
I become the author,
And the authority
In my own story
I become the absolute opposition
To what the colonial project predetermined
I return to myself
I become.

Excerpt from the text *Enquanto eu escrevo*, translated by Anne Quiangala, by the black Portuguese artist and theorist Grada Kilomba.

Inspired by the poem, try to write about yourself as the **protagonist,** that is, as the author of your own life. Only you know the best way to tell **your story.**

__/__/__

We invite you to begin writing your story with "I become. . ."

I become

My Fears

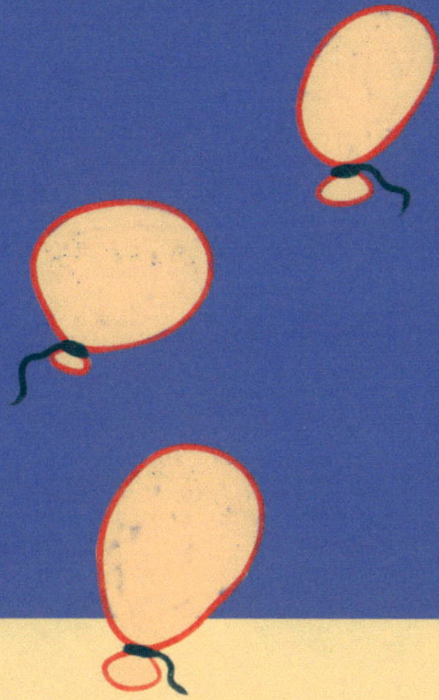

Imagine that you are filling balloons
with **your fears.**

Write your fears inside the balloons.

You can also draw **more ballons** on the page.

Now, pop the balloons.

How Are You?

Sometimes, we say, "I'm fine!" without really being fine. It's an automatic response.

Observe how you're feeling. If you want to and if you can, close your eyes and explore your feelings.

Observe your breathing. You don't need to breathe differently. Just pay attention. **How is it?**

Now, observe **your body**, all of it.

And how is **your mind?**

Fast?
Slow?

Tense?
Relaxed?

Silent?
Noisy?

Write here how you are feeling in your breathing, your body, and your mind.

My breathing is

__/__/__

Feelings in Jars

Put your feelings in these jars.

These feelings can spice up your writing or warm you up in the winter!

Inspired by the book *Uma página de cada vez (A Page Each Time)*.

__/__/__

Treasure Chest of Feelings

Imagine a moment of great joy
and let this sensation flood through your whole body.

Guard this feeling in your treasure chest.

Only you have the key to open it!

Words of Affection

Think of a **sentence** that has a feeling of hope, love, and protection.

Write this sentence.

Now say this sentence to 3 different people, without explaining anything.

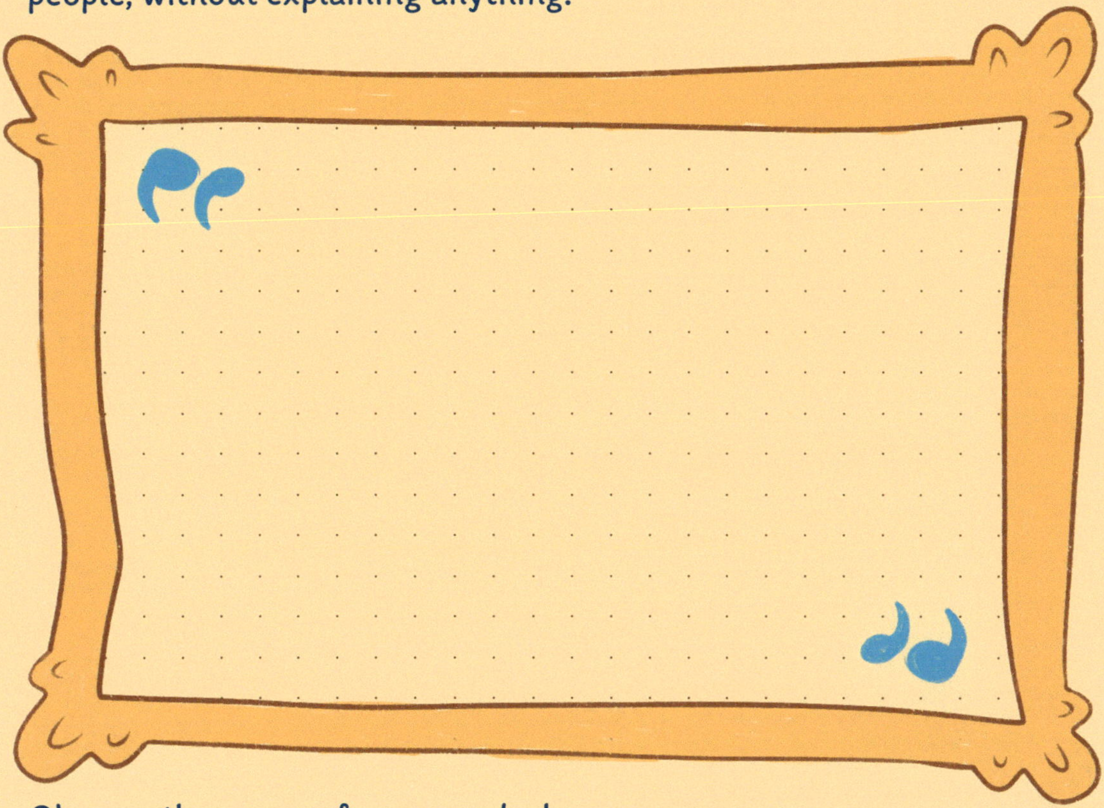

Observe the power of your words, how they can make someone's day better.

Repeat this exercise whenever you feel like it. Also, you don't need to have this workbook in your hands to do it.

Exercise inspired by *Livro de atividades: Mulheres possíveis (Possible Women: Workbook of Activities).*

__/__/__

Make a List Here of What Makes You Happy

It can be colors, animals, food, whatever makes you feel good.

1. Affection
2.
3.
4.

Our Feet

The feet are the surface on which **our body's weigh**t rests. Their shape is quite clever so that we can walk, dance, run and balance ourselves.

They deserve **special attention**, care, and pampering.

Let's move and feel our feet!

1 Sit in a position where you can comfortably **hold one of your feet.** You can also ask a partner to help you. First, do the entire exercise on just one foot.

2 **Stretch**, as if you have just woken up.

3 **Touch your foot** and feel the contact of your hands with the skin. Feel the textures, the softer parts, the thicker parts. Observe your foot to recognize all of it by touch.

4 **Massage the entire foot** as if you were kneading bread, with your entire hand.

5 Deepen the touch and **try to feel your bones.** Did you know that we have 26 bones in each foot? Take the opportunity to try to feel the shape of your bones.

6 Place your **fingers between your toes**, like a kind of hug between these parts of the body, creating space between your toes.

7 To finish, stand up, close your eyes and **feel the difference between your feet**, the one that has received a massage and the one that has not yet received one.

8 Now, let's go back to the first step to take care of the **other foot.**

Exercise inspired by Livro de atividades: Mulheres possíveis (Possible Women: Workbook of Activities).

 __/__/__

Where These Feet Have Already Walked

Where have your feet already **walked**?

What **places** have they been?

On the grass, the dirt, the sand,
on the trunks of trees,
on a cold floor, on a hot sidewalk,
on the moon, on the stars, on the sun?

Write or draw some of these places, whether they are real or imaginary.

My feet have already

__/__/__

If These Feet Could Talk

From the perspective of the feet, we are going to play with writing.
If your feet could **talk**, what would they say?
Where have they **walked**? Where do they want to go?
When did their steps **fail** them?
When were they on the **tips of their toes**?
When did they **plant** themselves and take **root**?

Write as if your feet were the authors of a story.

One time

Space

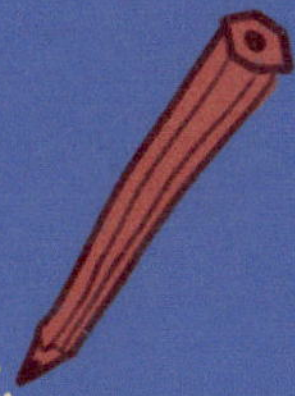

Observe your surroundings. **Choose a point** in your environment, such as an object, for example, and walk towards it. When you reach it, choose another one, and walk towards it.

Stay **close** and try to notice the details.

Stay **far away** and notice how your point of view changes your perception.

Let your gaze be **guided by the space**, like someone trying to recognize it. You can play with the levels: bend down, stand on tiptoe...

Now, imagine that you want to **describe** this place to someone who cannot see the place where you are...

Describe or draw this space.

__/__/__

Changes

Imagine you are a **place.**

What is it like?

What is it **needing**? A cleaning?
A shape? Reorganizing?

How would it be to **open** the windows?

Is today a beautiful day to **plant** new flowers
in this space?

What do you think about painting it? In what colors?

Describe or draw this space and what changes you would like to make to it.

__/__/__

The Magnifying Glass and the Telescope

The magnifying glass helps us see details in a **larger** size.

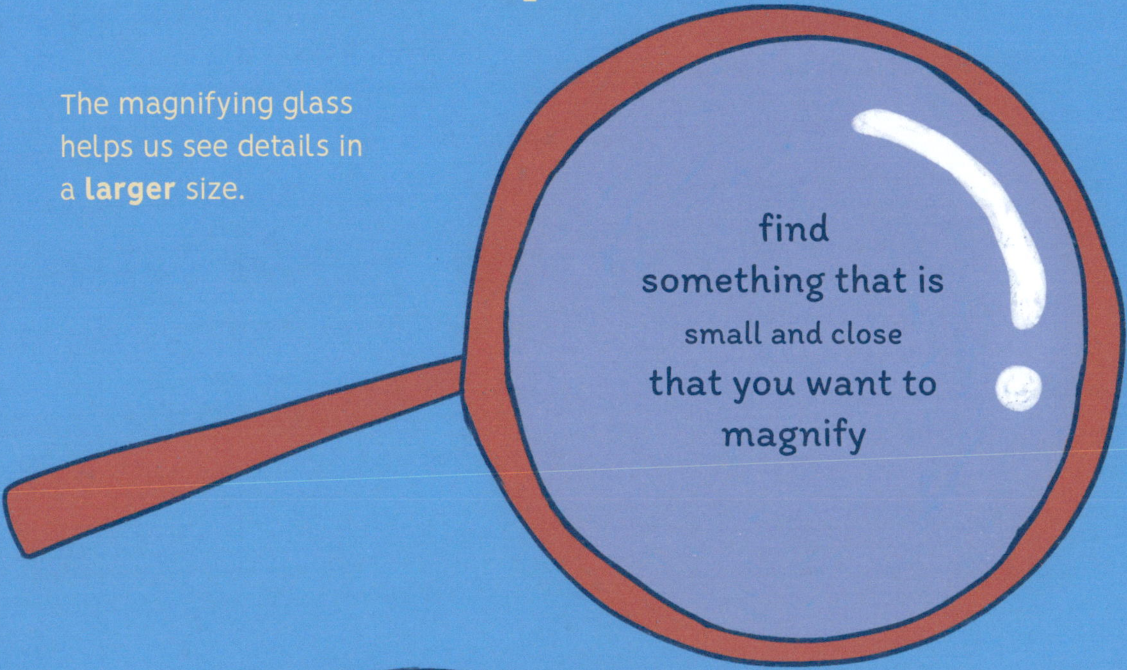

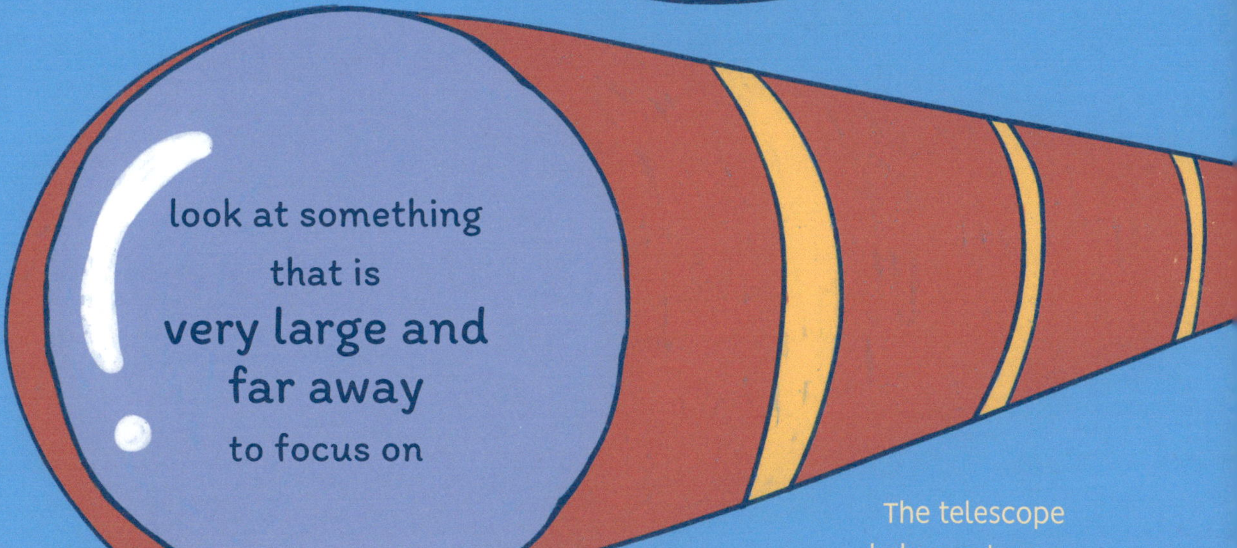

The telescope helps us to see distant things in **focus.**

Looking at Questions

When do I look at myself?
When do I look?
When am I looked at?
When do eyes touch?
When is a look a hug?
When do I communicate with a look?
When do I linger looking?
When do I look down?

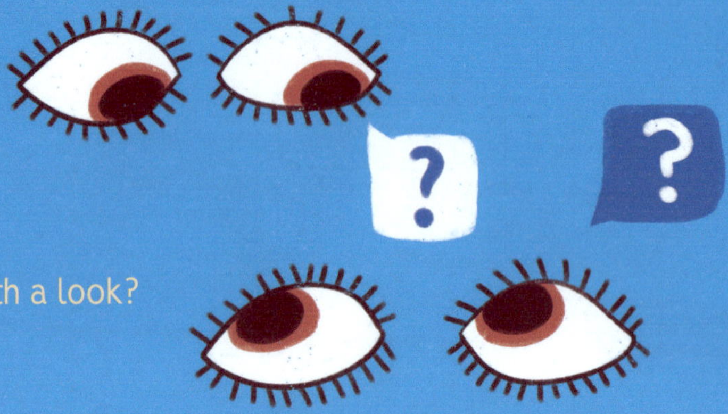

What other questions can we ask in this style?

Write more questions.

When do my eyes

The Touch of the Look

> *To look.*
> *Is an action.*
> *It is also a thing, the look.*
> *The look of someone who looks at us.*
> *The look of someone we observe*
> *while seeing something*
> *or someone else.*
> *It is an organ of F E E L I N G.*
> *Seeing, hearing, touching, smelling*
> *and tasting.*
> *Is it possible to touch someone with a look?*

Exercise inspired by Livro de atividades: Mulheres possíveis (Possible Women: Workbook of Activities).

Write or draw how you could touch someone with a look.

We can touch

__/__/__

To See with the Ears

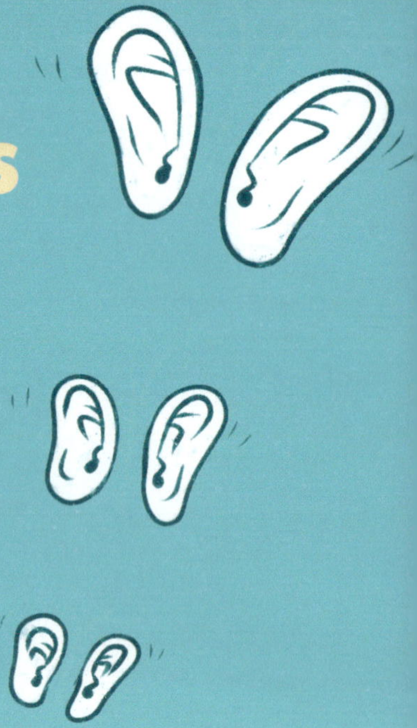

Close your eyes and try to **sharpen** your listening.

What do you hear?

Is it possible **to see** with your ears?

What if space were described **through sounds**?

If you could hear beyond **the walls that surround you**, what would you hear?

Which sounds are **closest** to you?

Which sounds are **farthest away**? Are there repetitive sounds? Are there human sounds?

Now describe the space where you are using the sounds that fill it.

__/__/__

Whispering Words

In our ears, we can...

... whisper words **softly...**

... shout words **loudly...**

... sing words with **melody...**

... declare words of **love...**

Add words to the drawings,

trying to convey different feelings.

Breathing Out

Inhale deeply through your nose. Exhale through your mouth, letting out a soft **AAAAAHHHHH** sound.

Once more.

Now, inhale while raising your shoulders, and when you exhale, let your shoulders relax.

Once more.

Let out a louder **AAAAAHHHHH**. You can open your mouth wider to do the exercise.

Imagine that when you exhale with this **AAAAAHHHHH**, you are throwing everything you no longer want out of your body.

Complete the drawing with everything you want to blow away from you.

__/__/__

Who Knows How to Listen?

> *I always see courses advertised on public speaking. I've never seen an ad for a course on listening. Everyone wants to learn how to speak. No one wants to learn how to listen. I thought about offering a course on listening. But I don't think anyone would sign up.*

Excerpt from the text *Escutatória*, by writer Rubem Alves

The author of the text jokes about how hard it is to listen. Why is that?

When do I **listen**?

Besides using my **ears**, how do I listen?

When do I **not** listen?

What do I **not** listen to?

When do others listen to **me**?

When do they **not** listen to **me**?

What do they **not** listen to?

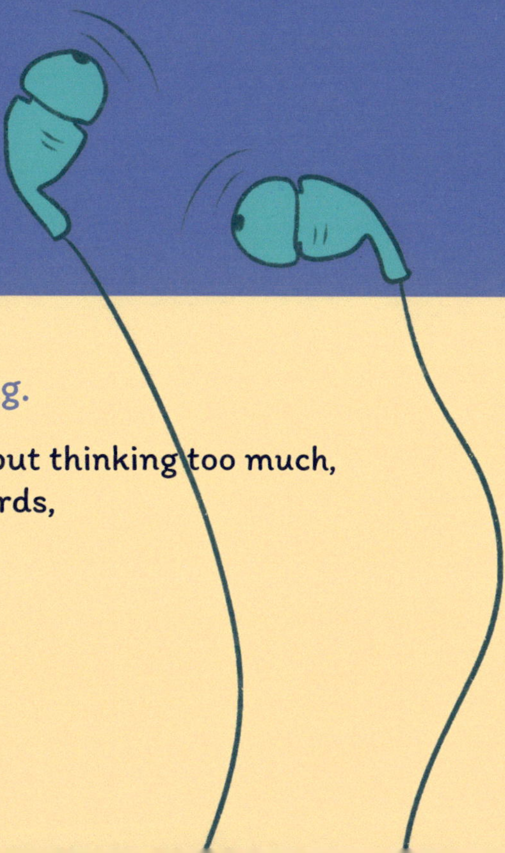

Listen to yourself and use the questions above to write something.

You can let the words come out without thinking too much, expressing them in lines or single words, in an abstract and disorganized way.

__/__/__

[●REC]

Backbone

This line of small bones that runs along our back is full of nerves, through which the spinal cord passes, and has tiny sacs of lubricating fluid between each of the vertebrae. Our spine is fully articulated, we can move it in many ways. It curls, extends, twists.

Have you ever had problems with pain, a stiff neck, or soreness in your spine? Let's be kind to our spines for a moment.

You can do this step by step on your own, or you can guide a friend.

1 To begin, touch the ends of the spine. It starts near the head. Carefully use your fingers to find where the first vertebra fits into the skull.

2 Then go to the other end and find the coccyx, which is the end of your tailbone.

3 Lie down on your bed or on a hard surface. Relax completely. Surrender to the earth, without fear, without holding on to anything. Just breathe, releasing your weight more and more towards the floor, and feel your entire spine, from your neck to your coccyx.

4 Go from lying down to sitting up, without stopping to feel your spine. When you are sitting all the way up, stabilize your weight firmly on your pelvis (hips). Try to stay as straight as possible, feeling the top of your head moving towards the sky. Observe how your body feels.

5 Pay attention to the way your feet feel, push the floor with them.

6 Stand up. Feel your spine aligned in this position and start moving, exploring all the movements that your spine can do. Drop your head and let your spine arch, turn back, try looking up, letting it stretch out completely. Look back, from one side to the other and feel the twists. Imagine that your spine is a snake, moving in various directions. Be free and experiment with joy and humor.

Exercise inspired by *Livro de atividades: Mulheres possíveis* (Possible Women: Workbook of Activities).

Describe what sensations you felt during this activity.

Write or draw.

Hands as Paintbrushes

> *Imagine that your hands are paintbrushes and that you are going to paint the space around you with vertical, horizontal, circular, spiral movements... Imagine or sing a song, alone or with a partner, and dance "painting the space" while moving to the rhythm of the song!*

Exercise inspired by Livro de atividades: Mulheres possíveis (Possible Women: Workbook of Activities).

Dance.

dance s l o w l y

dance with your eyes closed

dance quickly

dance in as weird a way as you can

dance on tiptoes

Making Faces

Let's move our faces.

Make as many different faces as you can.

Different expressions.

Smile.

Make big kisses.

Make baby kisses.

Imitate the sound of a fan, leaving your lips very loose: prprpr! vrvrrrrrr!

__/__/__

What Marks Us

> *Everything has, we all have, a face*
> *and marks. The dog and the snake*
> *and the seagulls and you and me,*
> *those who live and those who have lived*
> *and all who walk, crawl or fly:*
> *we all have a face and marks.*
> *The Mayans believe this.*
> *And they believe that the marks,*
> *invisible, are more face than the visible face.*
> *They know you by your mark.*

Eduardo Galeano

What are your visible and invisible marks?

Write in response to this question/reflection.

__/__/__

Words Can Heal

> *I write as if to save someone's life, probably my own.*
>
> Clarice Lispector

Inspired by this line by the author, imagine:

If words were medicine, what would they cure?

If words were capable of mending wounds, what would they be?

If words could fix someone's life, what would they say?

Write in response to these questions.

You can use single words, phrases, or verses.

If words heal. . .

__/__/__

Exploring the Head and Face

With your hands open, touch your face. Explore the touch on your entire head, noticing the shapes and textures.

With your hands open, as if you were messing up your hair, massage your scalp, trying to relax through touch. You can do it to yourself or invite a partner to do it.

Still touching the scalp, gently move your fingertips.

On your face, use your fingertips to feel different textures, identifying the physical shapes, the sizes, the temperature, everywhere you can feel.

Notice particulars shapes or sizes of parts of your face, go back to one of them. Why did that part catch your attention? Any memories? Does it feel good to touch?

Look for ways to move that part, as if you were molding clay. Notice if there has been any change. Is it more relaxed? Do you feel different?

Investigate the movements that cause you to relax. Massage your face, being kind to it, letting touch transform it.

__/__/__

Words in Boxes

Magda Lemonnier cuts out words
from newspapers, words of all sizes,
and keeps them in boxes.
In a red box she keeps the angry words.
In a green box, the loving words.
In a blue box, the neutral words.
In a yellow box, the sad words.
And in a transparent box she keeps
the words that have magic.
Sometimes she opens and turns the
boxes over on the table, so that the
words mix up in whatever way
they want. Then the words tell Magda
what happened and announce
what will happen.

Eduardo Galeano

You can also put your words in boxes.

 __/__/__

Neutral words

Loving words

Sad words

Angry words

Words that have magic

abracadabra

Meeting

Think of a **character.**
It could be an invented character, for example, a character from a soap opera you watch or a book you have read. But they could also be real, like a person you know.

Ask a friend to think of a **place**, real or imaginary.

Now, imagine that you **meet** this character in this place.

____

Write the name of the character here

____

Write the name of the place here

Write a scene with this character in this place.

— How nice to meet you here!

__/__/__

Somewhere

Ask a friend to name five different places.
It can be anywhere in the world or an imaginary place.
Now, ask them to name five actions (e.g. eating, walking).

List the places:

1. beach
2.
3.
4.
5.

List the actions:

1. tanning
2.
3.
4.
5.

Match each place to an action without repeating them.

Once you have five pairs, write a short story about each of them.

__/__/__

Word by Word, We Write Poetry

Ask someone to tell you five random words. Write these words down.

1.

2.

3.

4.

5.

Ask someone else to tell you five more words. List them here.

1.

2.

3.

4.

5.

Find one more person and ask them for five more words. Write them here.

1.

2.

3.

4.

5.

Look at these fifteen words and invent ways to put them together.

They can be short sentences or poetry. Don't think much about it. Just write fluidly, without judgment.

__/__/__

Improvising: Who? Where? What?

In the theatre we improvise
by asking WHO? WHERE? And WHAT?

For example: SOMEBODY and SOMEBODY ELSE (who) meet in PLACE (where) and SOMETHING HAPPENS (what).

Decide who the people are in your story, where it takes place, and what happens.

Write the story that comes out of these choices.

Once upon a time. . .

__/__/__

A Story in 7 Steps

Now we're going to play with writing a story in **seven steps**.

Use these seven items to write a story, filling in the gaps.

The story can be real or invented, or it can be real and invented at the same time.

The steps are:

1. There was a time

2. And everyday

3. Until one day

4. And then, because of this

5. And also because of this

6. Until finally

7. It was like this

__ /__ /__

Life Histories

Ask someone to tell you a **story** that they lived through. Pay close attention.

Then rewrite this story.
You can mix in your own narrative.

You can change the characters, the places, the dates, and even what is real or fictional.

Step 1: **Try to write as if you were telling the story to someone.**

Step 2: **Try to write as if you were the protagonist in the story, as if the story were your own.**

__/__/__

Memories

Now think about a story of **your own**.

A **memory** is an act of creation in the present.

In the present we give **significance** to the past, enabling ourselves to **construct** other narratives apart from those that **happened to us.**

Use your memories to write a text for the present moment.

New meanings and motivations may emerge out of what has already happened.

I remember. . .

__/__/__

Time Machine

If you had a time machine,
where would you want to go?
It could be a moment or a place.

Write about this.

I would go to . . .

Why Do I Write?

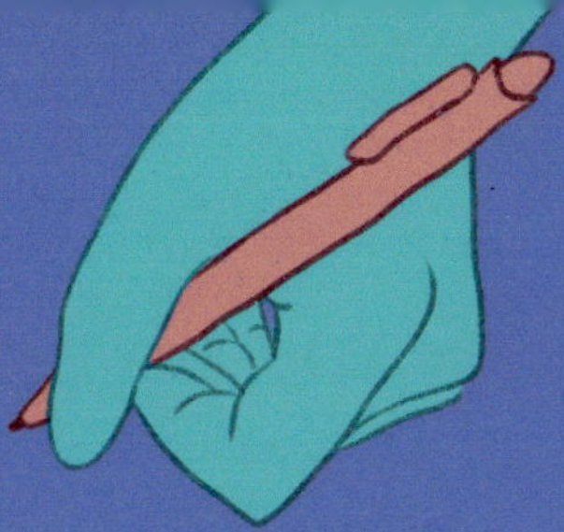

> *Why am I driven to write? Because I have no choice. Because I must keep the spirit of my revolt alive, and myself, too. Because the world I create in writing makes up for what the real world does not give me. In writing, I bring order to the world, I give it a handle so I can hold it. I write because life does not appease my appetites and my hunger. I write to record what others erase when I speak, to rewrite the poorly written stories about me. To become more intimate by myself and with myself. To discover myself, preserve myself, build myself, achieve autonomy. To convince myself that I have value and that what I have to say is not a load of crap. To show that I can and that I will write, regardless of the warnings to the contrary. Finally, I write because I am afraid of writing, but I am even more afraid of not writing.*
>
> Gloria Anzaldúa, Chicana writer and theorist

Write your reflections based on your reading of the text. How did it touch you? What are the connections you can make with the author's words?

Tell us what drives you to write.

I write because. . .

(Re)Starting

We began our first journey in this book with a wish for our future. Something ends so that something else can begin. An end full of (re)starts.

> *Imagine living in a world where there is no domination, where women and men [and trans and non-binary people] are not alike or even always the same, but where the notion of mutuality is the ethos* that determines our interaction. Imagine living in a world where we can all be who we are, a world of peace and possibility. A feminist revolution alone will not create that world; we need to end racism, elitism, imperialism. But it will make it possible for us to be self-actualized people—women and men, [transgender people, regardless of sexual orientation]—who can create a loving community, live together, realize our dreams of freedom and justice, and live the truth that we are all 'created equal.' Come closer. See how feminism can touch and change your life and the lives of all of us. Come closer and learn, at the source, what the feminist movement is. Come closer and you will see: feminism is for everyone.*

bell hooks, African American scholar

*ethos, a Greek word, meaning a set of customs and habits of behavior and culture characteristic of a given community, time, or region.

Imagine your ideal world and write about it here. Let your words flow. Let it come out like a dream, without thinking too much. Just imagine your better world.

This exercise was inspired by an activity book in Portuguese called *Mulheres possíveis* (Possible Women).

How Was Your Experience?

Reflecting on your writing process can be a good way to prepare yourself to write more in future.

Here are a few questions to help you think about how you experienced writing as you worked your way through this book.

What did you think was **most interesting** in this book? Why?

Did you have any **trouble** with any of the exercises? Which one(s)?

What part(s) did you **not enjoy** doing? Why?

What would make you **enjoy writing more**?

Write about it here. See if you find any good strategies for doing more writing in future.

__/__/__

These two pages are purposefully blank, open for you to fill in any way you desire: drawing, writing, making notes, writing poems or stories.

Enjoy this space of your own!